Gorgons

by J. K. Anderson
Professor of Classical Archaeology
in the University of California, Berkeley
Line drawings from the antiquities by Nancy Conkle

The front cover is from a terracotta metope, c. 600 B.C. Syracuse; the back cover is from a stand by Kleitias, c. 570 B.C. The Metropolitan Museum of Art

From a black-figure dinos by the Gorgon Painter, c. 600 B.C. Louvre

From a red-figure hydria by the Berlin Painter, Munich

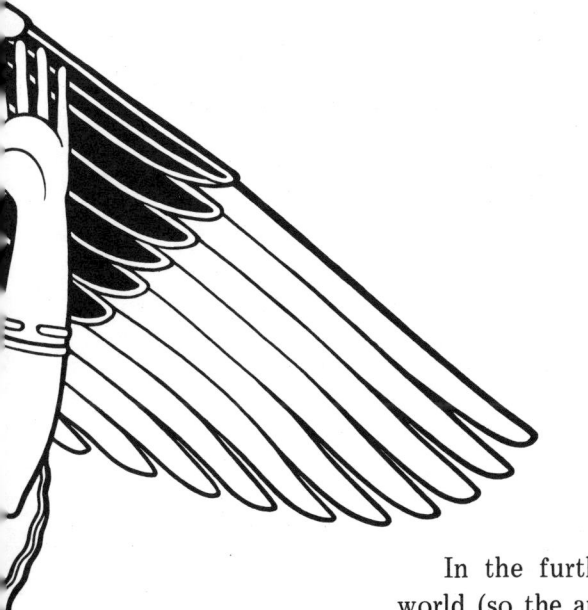

THE STORY OF THE
Gorgons

In the furthest west, beyond the stream of Ocean that encircled the world (so the ancient Greeks believed) lay the magic island where the three sister Gorgons lived. They were the daughters of Phorcys, the Old Man of the Sea, and of Ceto, a dragon of the deep. Two of them, Stheno the Mighty and Euryale, the Far-leaping, were immortal; but the third, Medusa the Queen, was fated to die. Medusa was beloved of Poseidon, who was lord of the sea, and among the gods of the Greeks second only to his brother Zeus the Thunderer. You may well be surprised at this when you see the Gorgons in this book, with their huge round faces fringed with serpents instead of locks of hair; their great goggling eyes; their mouths stretching in gigantic grins from side to side of their faces; their huge teeth, and dangling tongues. The poets explain this puzzle by saying that Medusa had once been beautiful (and I suppose her sisters were too). But she boasted of Poseidon's love, and the gods punished her by making her hideous — so hideous that the mere sight of her eyes was enough to turn a man to stone. Even this punishment did not content her chief enemy, the goddess Athena; and Athena resolved to bring about Medusa's death.

Now there was living on the little Greek island of Seriphos a fisher-lad named Perseus. Years before, an old fisherman named Dictys, "the Net," had drawn from the sea a great wooden chest. To his astonishment, he found inside it a beautiful girl, with a little baby boy sleeping upon her breast. This boy was Perseus, a prince and more than a prince, if his story had been known.

For his mother Danae was daughter of the great King Acrisius of Argos. Danae was the king's only child, and he was seeking some prince to be her husband when a warning came to him from the gods that she would some day bear a son who would cause her father's death. So Acrisius gave up all thought of his daughter's marriage, and shut her up in a prison-chamber whose only opening was in the roof high above her.

But the purposes of the gods were not to be turned aside. Through this opening Zeus himself, the Thunderer, descended in the form of a shower of gold, which Danae caught up in her bosom. And presently the little boy Perseus was born, the son of the Thunder-god and the princess.

Danae & the Rain of Zeus

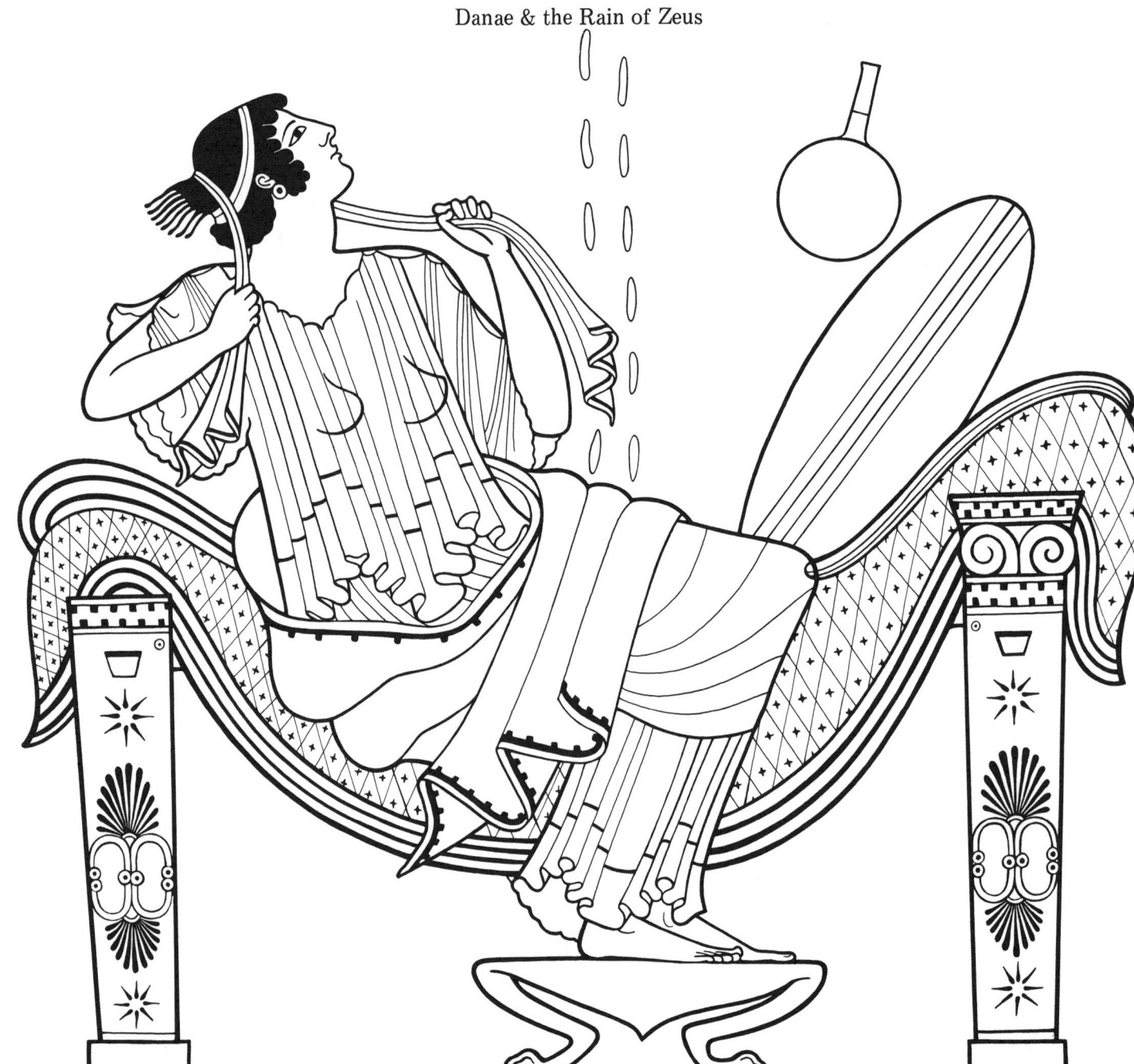

From a red-figure calyx crater by the Triptolemos Painter, Leningrad, Hermitage

From a red-figure hydria by the Gallatin Painter, Museum of Fine Arts, Boston

When Acrisius learned of the child's birth, he ordered a great wooden chest to be made, and shut Danae and Perseus inside it, and had them thrown into the sea to drift at the mercy of the winds and waves, thinking that this would be an end of them — as it would have been, if the gods had not guided the chest to Seriphus, where it was brought to shore by old Dictys.

Now Dictys himself was not what he seemed, but the rightful king of the island, who had been driven from his throne by his brother Polydectes and sent to live as best he could in a poor hut on a distant rocky headland. Indeed, so distant was it that it was not until Perseus was grown into a young man that Polydectes learned about the beautiful woman whom his brother had rescued, and cared for as if she had been his own daughter.

Polydectes resolved to take Danae, against her will, to be his wife. But first Perseus must be put out of the way. For this purpose, the king held a great feast, at which his nobles presented him with costly gifts. At last Perseus, who was among the guests, was called on for his gift, and since he was so poor, he had nothing to bring. But, sooner than letting himself be shamed before the company, he shouted to Polydectes that he would bring him the greatest gift of all, the head of Medusa the Gorgon. Then he left the palace and wandered along the barren sea shore, knowing that he could never return without accomplishing his boast but having little idea how this was to be done.

From the Temple of Artemis, Corfu, early 6th century B.C.

From a South Italian crater, British Museum

Suddenly there stood before him a woman, helmeted and armed with shield and spear, but taller and more beautiful than any mortal woman. She told him that in order to carry out the task that he had laid on himself he must go first to the Grey Women, sisters of the Gorgons, who had but one eye and one tooth between them. If Perseus could seize the eye and the tooth, they would tell him the way to the Nymphs, who would give him gifts, without which he would never be able to overcome Medusa. Then she vanished, and Perseus knew that he had been talking to the goddess Athena herself.

After long wandering, he came to the desolate shore in the far west where the Grey Women lived. Creeping up behind them, he seized their one eye as they were passing it from hand to hand, and, when they began to quarrel about who had it, possessed himself of their tooth also. Long and loud they screeched when they learned that they must starve in blindness if they did not do the will of a mortal man; but there was no help for it, and at last they sent Perseus to the Nymphs. From them, he received winged sandals that would carry him over the ocean to the Gorgons' island; a cap of darkness that would make him invisible; and a magic bag in which to carry off Medusa's head. To cut it off, Hermes the messenger god furnished him with a curved blade, shaped like a sickle, and so sharp that it would cut through anything at a single blow.

From a black-figure cup by Psiax, Hermitage

Now at last he came, flying swiftly through the air, to the island where the three sister Gorgons lay sleeping. The serpents in their hair hissed and wriggled, but they themselves did not stir as the invisible hero approached, turning his face away, for he knew well the power of the Gorgons' eyes. Some people say that Athena gave him a polished shield, which he used as a mirror, and so guided his blow, but the Greek artists who made the first pictures of the story do not show this, as you can see from this book.

From a South-Italian red-figure amphora, c. 330 B.C. Berlin, *Staatliche Museen*

But just now there was no time for curiosity. A single stroke of his blade severed Medusa's neck, and at once he thrust the head into his bag, sprang into the air, and was off as fast as his winged sandals could carry him. There was need for haste, because Stheno and Euryale had been awakened, and

From a limestone metope from Sicily, c. 530 B.C. Archaeological Museum, Palermo

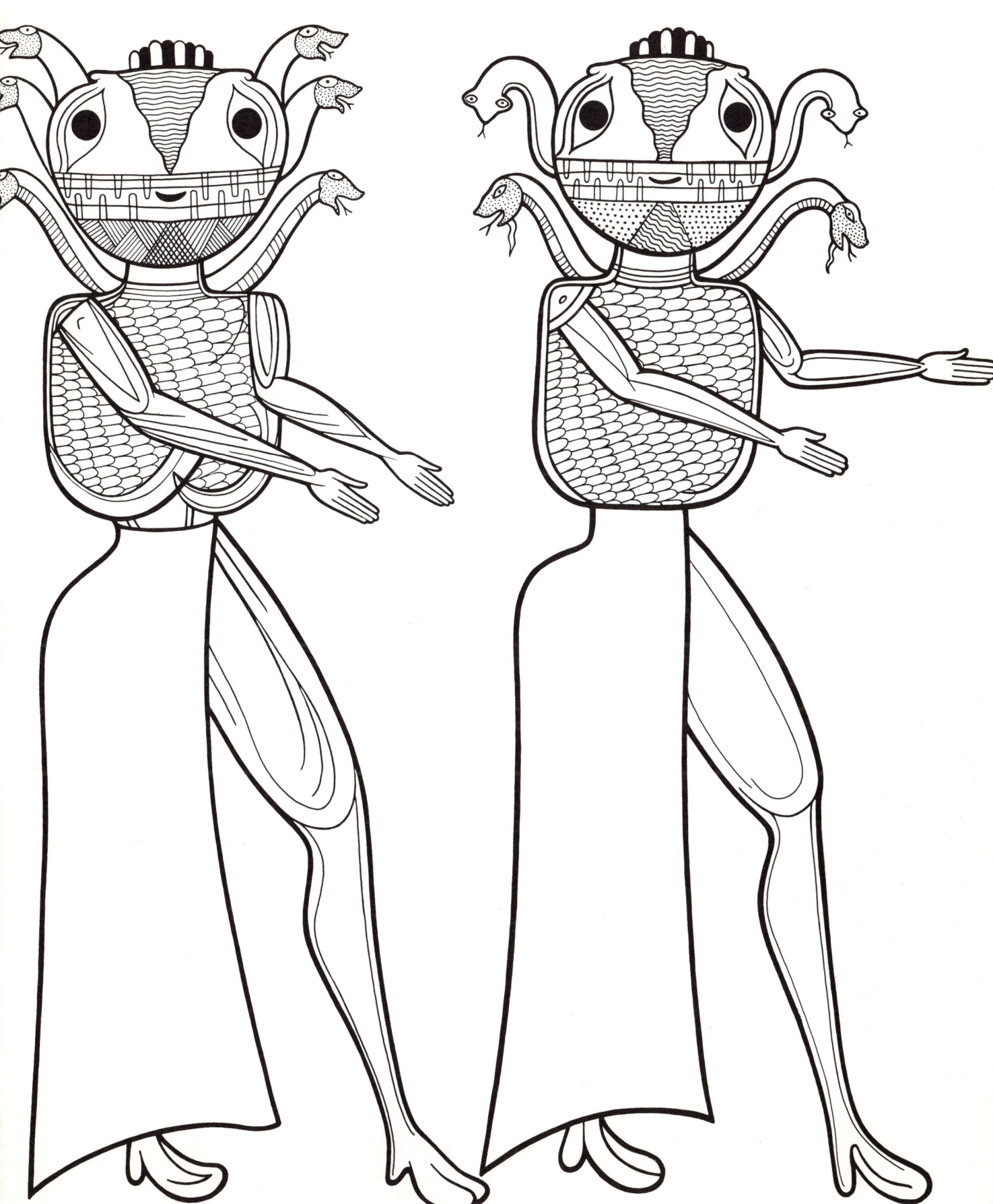

From an Attic amphora, c. 670 B.C. Eleusis Museum

rushed after their sister's slayer, whom they followed like bloodhounds, invisible though he was. But, whether Athena came between them and Perseus, or whether Perseus himself was too fast for them, they were forced to give up the pursuit, and we hear no more of them, except that Athena, when she invented the flute, copied upon it the sound of their wailing.

From a red-figure hydria by the Pan Painter, c. 470 B.C. British Museum

From an amphora by the Nettos Painter, c. 600 B.C. National Museum, Athens

15

From an amphora by the Nettos Painter, c. 600 B.C. National Museum, Athens

From the body of Medusa there sprang, through the severed neck, her children, the sons of Poseidon, Chrysaor of the golden sword and Pegasus, the winged horse, whom Bellerophon tamed. But their stories do not concern us.

From an Attic black-figure lekythos by the Diosphos painter, c. 480 B.C. The Metropolitan Museum of Art

17

From a Cypriot sarcophagus, early 5th century B.C. The Metropolitan Museum of Art

Perseus flew on and on over the ocean, knowing that the world from which he came lay somewhere far toward the sunrise. At last a shadowy form appeared above the horizon, and as he drew nearer he saw that it was a gigantic old man, bowed under an immense burden. His head rose to the clouds; his feet reached the breaking surf. Forests clothed his shoulders, and

From a dinos by the Gorgon Painter, Louvre

his hair and beard were stiff with crackling ice. This was Atlas, the giant who bore the heavens on his shoulders, and well he knew the story of the Gorgons and the purpose of the hero's errand. As Perseus flew past, Atlas called out to him to hold up the head of Medusa. As soon as he looked upon it, he was turned to stone and freed forever from the pain of his burden. Still at this day Mount Atlas stands in North Africa, with its snow-covered head seeming to rise to the skies.

From a dinos by the Gorgon Painter, c. 600 B.C. Louvre

On and on flew Perseus, far above the burning deserts of Africa, and as he went the blood dripped from the bag in which he was carrying the head. Each drop, as it touched the sands, turned into a poisonous snake, and the desert swarms with these reptiles to this day.

From a terracotta metope from the temple of Apollo at Thermon, c. 620 B.C. National Museum, Athens

At last Perseus came to the sea coast of the land of the Ethiopians, and saw below him a strange sight — a beautiful girl, chained to a rock at the water's edge, and a sorrowing crowd watching her from a distance. All at once there was a swirl in the water off shore; a monstrous head broke the

From a terracotta metope from the temple of Apollo at Thermon, c. 620 B.C. National Museum, Athens

ANDROMEDA from a South Italian pelike, Naples

surface, and with gaping jaws made straight for the girl. But swifter still Perseus swooped down, with Medusa's head in his outstretched hand. At the sight, the monster was turned to stone, and travellers say that it still lies in the sea, a great reef of rock with the waves breaking over it.

Now a few quick slashes with the blade of sharpness set the girl free, and Perseus learned her story from her own lips. She was Andromeda, the daughter of the king and queen of Ethiopia, and her mother had foolishly boasted that she was more beautiful than the sea-nymphs. So the gods had sent the monster to lay waste the land, and told the king and queen that the only way of deliverance was to chain their daughter to the rock for the monster to devour. Perseus restored the princess to her parents, and needless to say she became his bride, though only after he had used Medusa's head once more, to dispose of a rival.

PERSEUS from a South Italian pelike, Naples

The Gorgon is shown as mistress of wild beasts, from the front of an Etruscan chariot of the sixth century B.C. Since the man who made this picture was not Greek, we do not know whether he was thinking of Medusa

at all, or showing one of the demons that belonged to his own people's stories. At all events, he produced a terrifying monster, to keep away bad luck from the chariot and the men who rode in it.

From a bronze relief from an Etruscan chariot, Munich, *Alte Pinakothek*

Now Perseus returned to Seriphus, taking Andromeda with him. He arrived in the nick of time, just as the wicked Polydectes and his courtiers were about to begin the wedding feast to celebrate the king's marriage to poor Danae. Perseus entered the palace hall alone and travel-stained, looking not at all like a conquering hero, and Polydectes called out mockingly from his high seat, to ask if he had brought the Gorgon's head. "Behold!" cried Perseus, and at once a silence fell on that boisterous company, which was never to be broken. King and revellers were frozen into stones; and so powerful was the spell that they say that even the frogs of Seriphus have been silent and given up croaking from that day to this.

Top: from a gold ring from Smyrna, British Museum; bottom: from a bronze hydria, Field Museum, Chicago

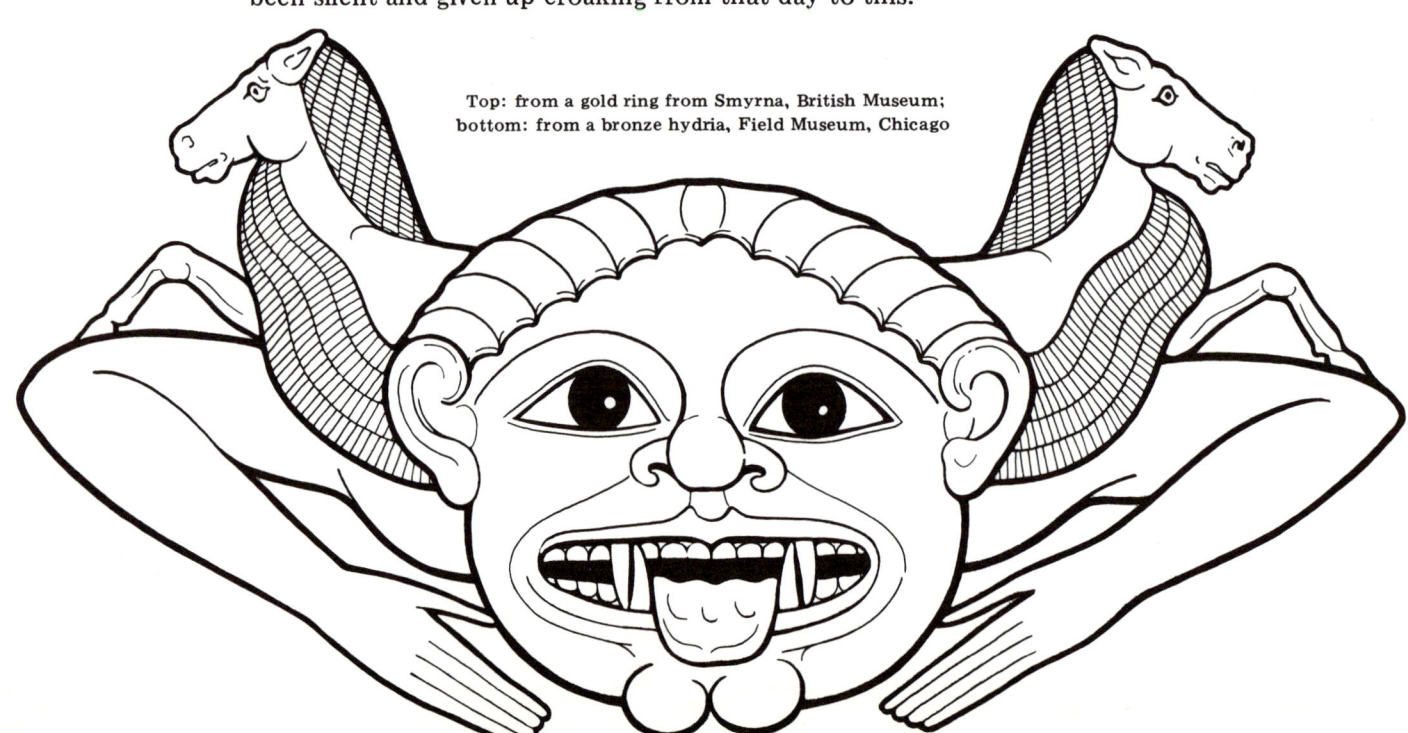

Now Perseus restored old Dictys to the kingdom that was rightly his, and set off with Danae and Andromeda for Argos. He meant no harm to his grandfather, but Acrisius was terrified when he heard of his grandson's coming and fled away to Thessaly. Perseus followed and found the old man judging the athletes at the games in honor of a dead king. Wishing to prove his might before he made himself known to his grandfather, Perseus picked up a discus and hurled it far beyond the mark set by the other competitors. But a gust of wind caught it, and it struck the forehead of Acrisius, who fell dead, slain by his daughter's son as the gods had warned him.

From a red-figure pelike by the Pan Painter, Munich, *Antikensammlungen*

Perseus was curious to know what Medusa really looked like, and asked Athena to find some way for him to see her face without being turned into stone. She said that he could look at Medusa's reflection, but not at the head itself. So here Perseus stands, with one foot on a rock at whose foot is a pool of water surrounded by large pebbles. Athena is sitting on a bank above the other side of the pool. The bank itself is not shown, but the goddess' shield leans against it, below a young olive tree. (Athena gave the olive tree to mankind and it was sacred to her.) I think that she is holding a flute in her left hand. She invented the flute; its notes were like the wailing of Medusa's

From an Apulian crater, 4th century B.C. Gotha

sisters. Her right hand is stretched high above the pool, and she holds Medusa's head by the hair. This is a much more human Gorgon than most of the others in this book, but the eyes are still dangerous and Perseus is looking downwards, towards the rather dim reflection in the pool.

⟵ This picture was painted on a wine-bowl by a Greek living in South Italy towards the end of the fourth century B.C. At this time the Greeks were very fond of the theatre, and this scene probably comes from a play which was forgotten soon after it was written. We do not know the author's name.

From an Etruscan architectural terracotta, c. 500 B.C. The J. Paul Getty Museum

From a red-figure amphora by the Andokides Painter, Berlin

After this Perseus did not go back to Argos, but founded the great city of Mycenae, where his secret spring can be seen to this day. As for the head of Medusa, some people say that he buried it in the market-place at Argos. But most people are agreed that he gave it to Athena, who wears it on her aegis, the magic cloak with which she shelters her friends and terrifies her enemies.

A shield from a red-figure amphora, c. 500 B.C. British Museum

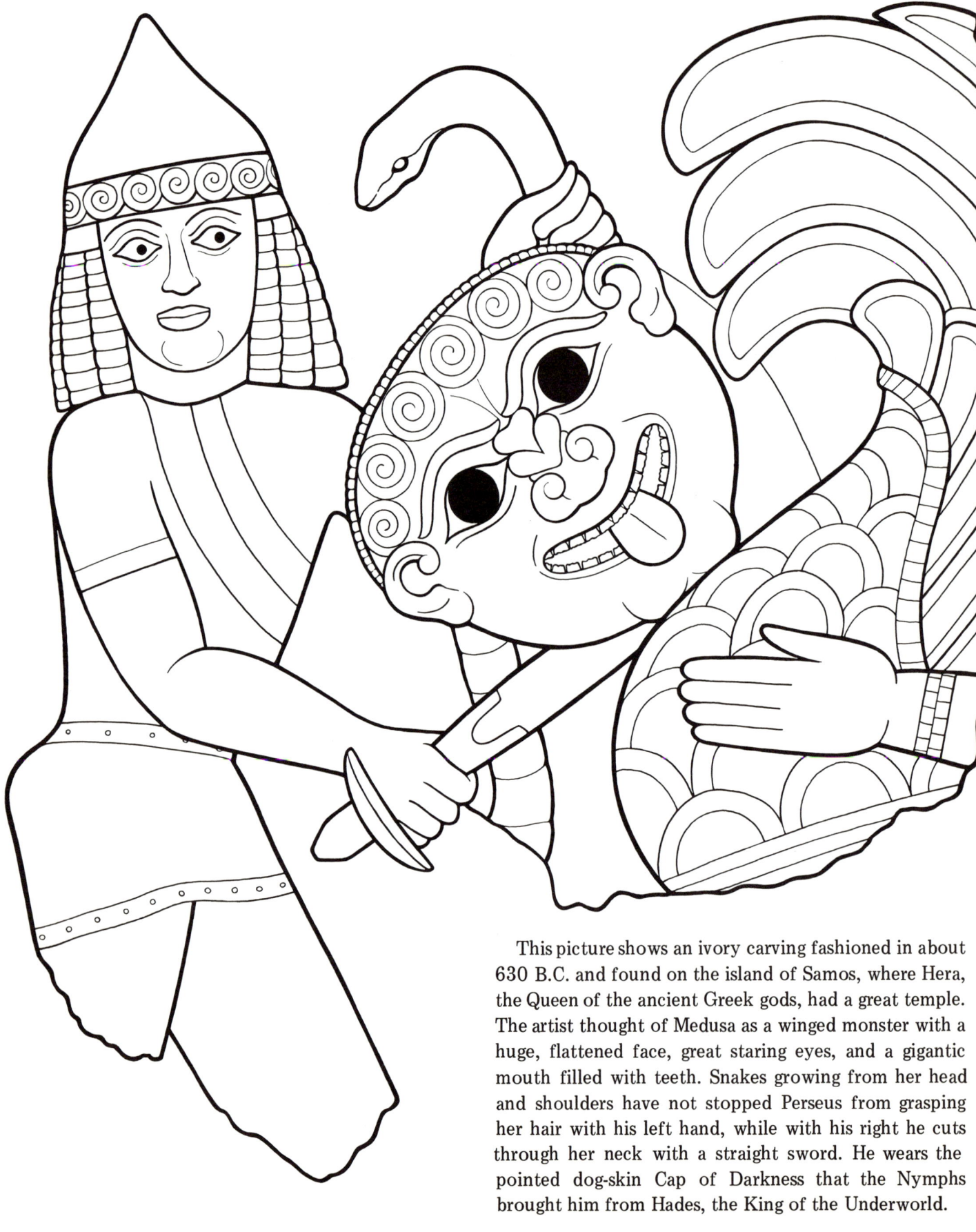

This picture shows an ivory carving fashioned in about 630 B.C. and found on the island of Samos, where Hera, the Queen of the ancient Greek gods, had a great temple. The artist thought of Medusa as a winged monster with a huge, flattened face, great staring eyes, and a gigantic mouth filled with teeth. Snakes growing from her head and shoulders have not stopped Perseus from grasping her hair with his left hand, while with his right he cuts through her neck with a straight sword. He wears the pointed dog-skin Cap of Darkness that the Nymphs brought him from Hades, the King of the Underworld.

From an ivory fragment from Samos, c. 630 B.C. Samos Museum

33

From a chalcedony seal from Kerch, Leningrad

Medusa seems wide awake here and is running away from Perseus, who has seized her by the back hair and plunged his sword of sharpness into her neck. He does not seem to be troubled by the snakes in her hair, or by the even bigger ones round her waist. But he is careful to turn his head away, so that the sight of her eyes will not turn him into stone. On the right, Hermes, the messenger of the gods, stands by. He shows that all the gods are pleased with what Perseus is doing, and he has an important job to do himself. He will lead Medusa's ghost away into the dark home of Hades, the ruler of the dead, beneath the earth. The long stick that he carries, with little snakes twisting at its end, is a herald's staff, to show that he carries messages from the gods, and he also uses it to guide the ghosts.

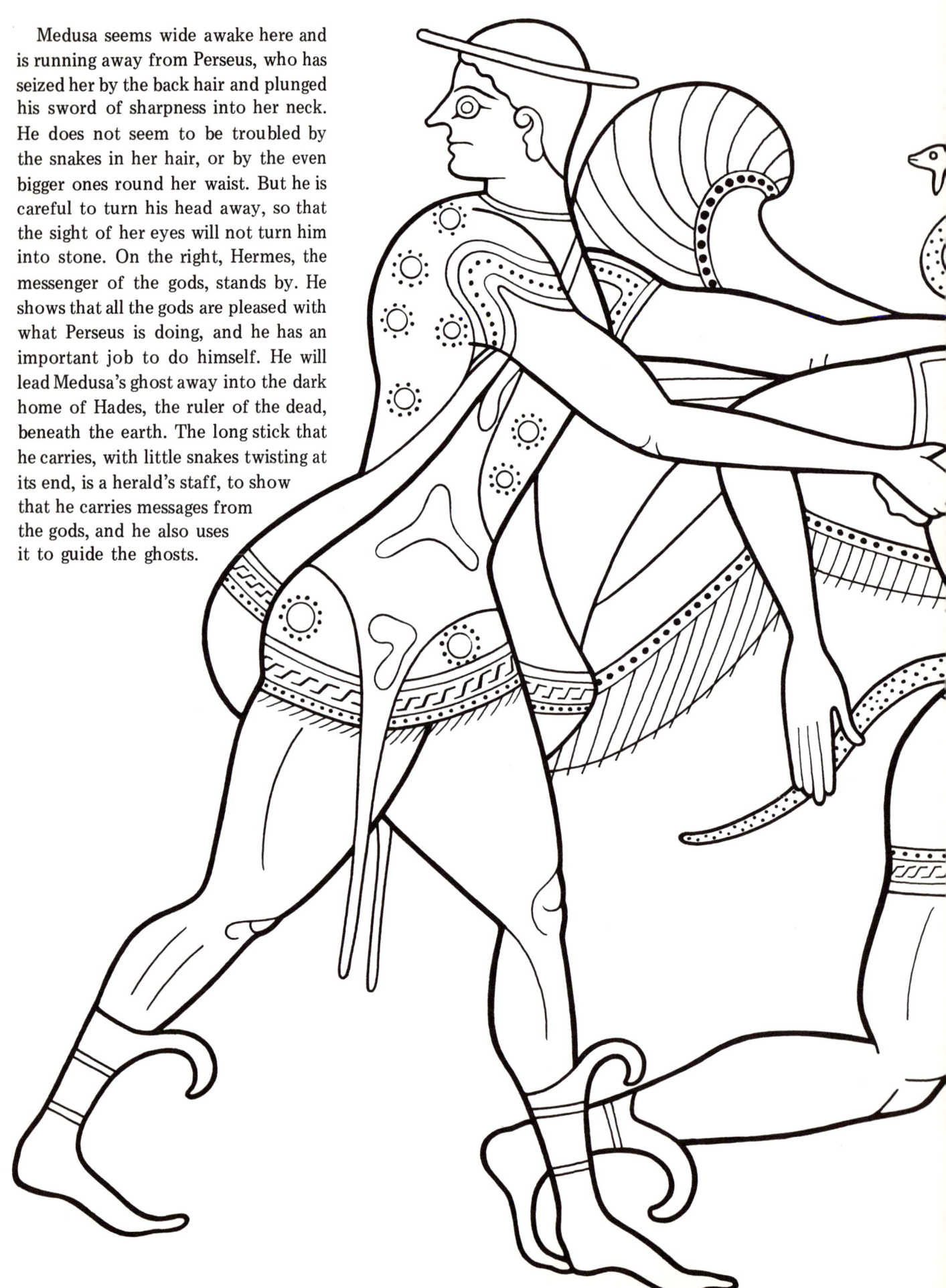

From a black-figure olpe by the Amasis Painter, c. 530 B.C. British Museum

Some of the Roman poets said that Perseus did not fly with his winged sandals, but rode away on Pegasus. In the Middle Ages more people read Latin than Greek, and so this became the usual version of the story. To Christine de Pisan, a poetess who lived at the time of the Hundred Years War between France and England, Perseus was "like a good knight errant," and that is how he was painted by an artist who illustrated a book of her poems in about 1415 A.D. Perseus, from his helmet to his golden spurs, is equipped like the French knights who fought the battle of Agincourt, and Pegasus is armored like their chargers, and has the same sort of saddle. However, Perseus does not wield a knightly lance or sword, but a great scythe, with which he is about to slash off the head of the monster, who is coming out of the sea just below the rock where Andromeda stands. Andromeda is saying her prayers, but she seems quite calm, as though she knows that they will be answered. She is dressed like a fashionable young lady of Christine's time.

From chalcedony seals, top: British Museum; bottom: Bowdoin College

37

From Christine de Pisan, British Museum MS. Harley 4431, c. 1410

This picture, painted on a plate made in the island of Rhodes in about 600 B.C., may perhaps help to explain one of the most puzzling things about Medusa — her name. The literal meaning of Medusa is "She who rules," but in the story she is a forlorn creature, betrayed and accursed by the gods, and her two sisters, with whom she shares her desert island, do not seem to be her subjects.

British Museum

←— But on this plate she shows a lively leg as a self-satisfied "Mistress of Wild Things," with an unfortunate water fowl grasped in either hand. Artemis, the goddess of wild animals, is sometimes drawn in very much the same way, and perhaps the artist who painted this plate thought of Medusa as one of the terrifying powers of nature which in some way govern and enrich life even by their own deaths.

The cross on her leg, and the rosettes of dots on her arms and on her thigh, look as though they ought to be tattoos, and signs of her magical power. But I think they are only decorative patterns, like the bigger ones in the background.

From a bronze tripod leg, Olympia Museum

About twenty-six hundred years ago some Greek warrior fixed this splendid monster, cut out of a bronze sheet and engraved, to the front of his shield. When he grew old, he hung his shield up as a gift to the gods in the great sanctuary at Olympia. Or perhaps he was killed in battle and his enemies picked up the shield on the battlefield and hung it up as a memorial of their victory.

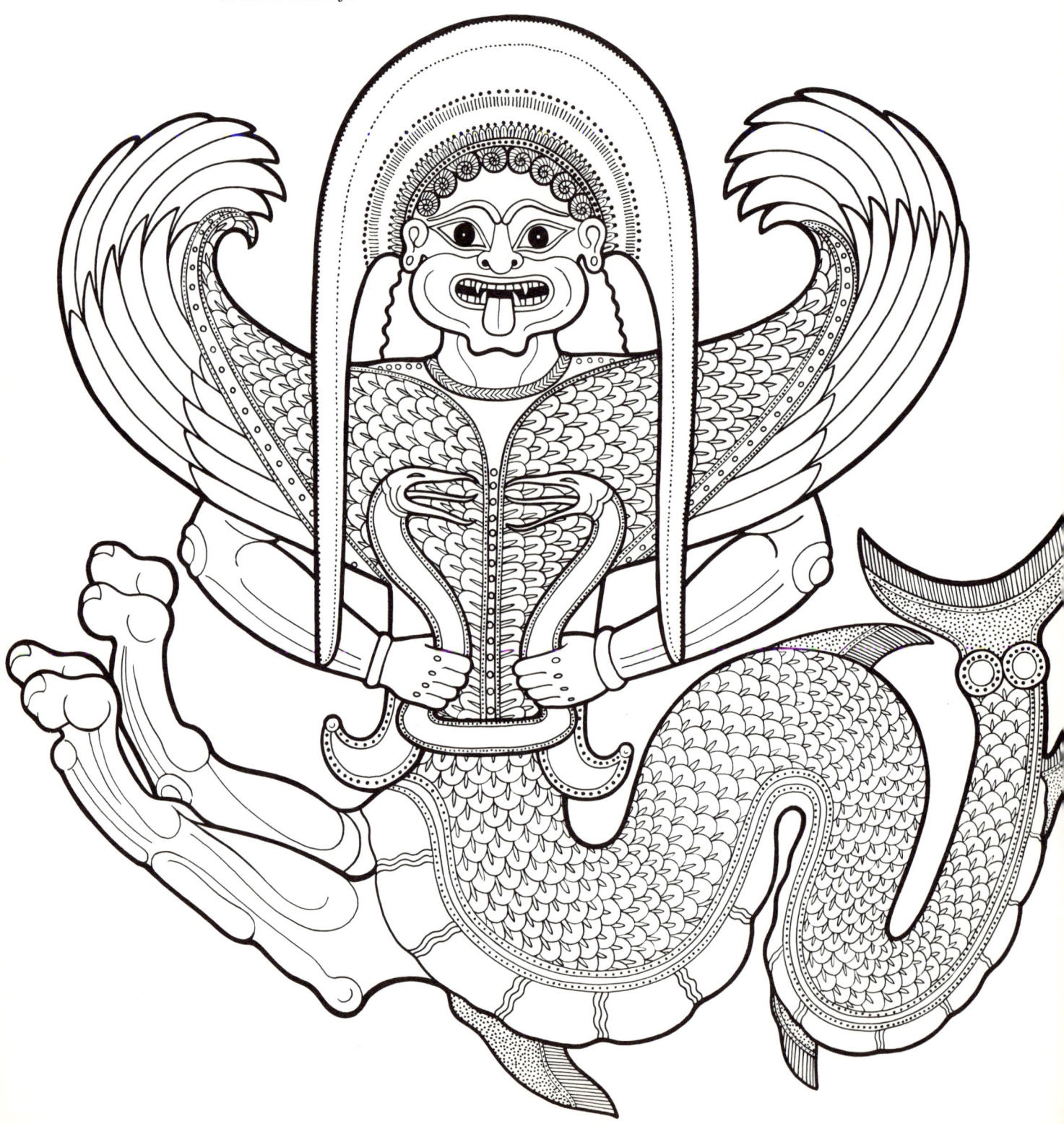

From a bronze shield plate, mid-6th century B.C. Olympia Museum

We cannot be quite certain that the monster on page 40 is Medusa the Gorgon. She may be some sort of fearsome mermaid, a bane to mariners. But the face, wings and serpent-girdle are Medusa's, and the huge fishy tail reminds us that Medusa's parents were sea-creatures, and that she was loved by Poseidon, the Lord of the Sea. She has a lion's front legs and claws, to seize her prey.

Here, however, there is no doubt at all that Medusa is intended, since she clasps her children, Pegasus the winged horse and Chrysaor, under her arms. The artist, like many other early Greek artists, is not troubled by the thought that Chrysaor and Pegasus were not born until Perseus cut off Medusa's head and her children sprang into the world from her neck.

This picture was hammered out and engraved on a bronze strip, about four inches wide, that was fastened inside a shield in order to secure the band through which the warrior who carried it passed his left arm. It was found at Olympia, like the blazons, and was made about the same time, perhaps about 550 B.C.

From a bronze shield strap, Olympia Museum

From an amphora from Boeotia, early 7th century B.C. Louvre

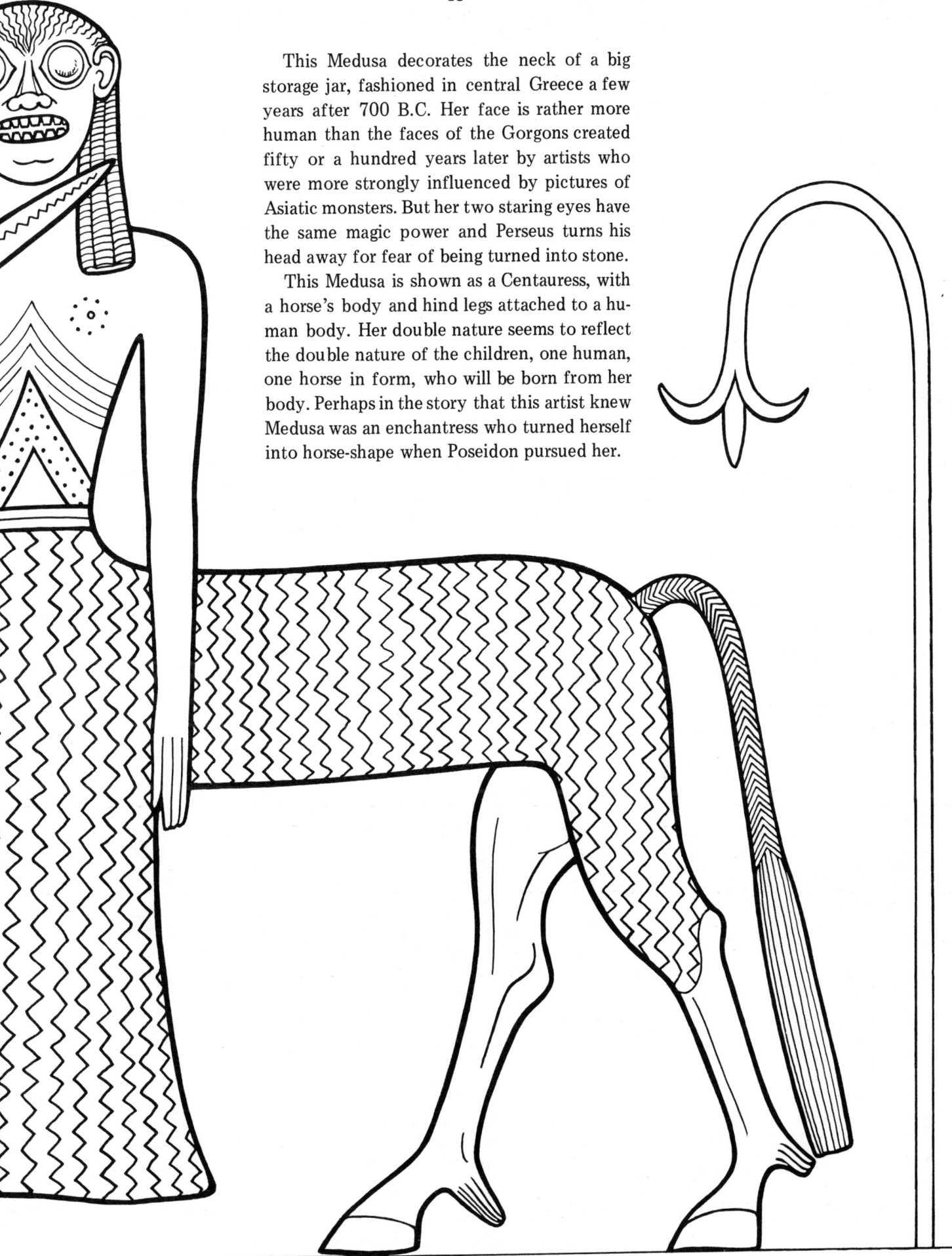

This Medusa decorates the neck of a big storage jar, fashioned in central Greece a few years after 700 B.C. Her face is rather more human than the faces of the Gorgons created fifty or a hundred years later by artists who were more strongly influenced by pictures of Asiatic monsters. But her two staring eyes have the same magic power and Perseus turns his head away for fear of being turned into stone.

This Medusa is shown as a Centauress, with a horse's body and hind legs attached to a human body. Her double nature seems to reflect the double nature of the children, one human, one horse in form, who will be born from her body. Perhaps in the story that this artist knew Medusa was an enchantress who turned herself into horse-shape when Poseidon pursued her.

This shield-blazon, found at Olympia, shows the Gorgon within three whirling wings, as one of the Powers of the Air. Monstrous faces or masks have been used in many parts of the world to terrify human enemies and to ward off supernatural powers.

From a bronze shield ornament, first half of the 6th century B.C., Olympia Museum

Bulgarian National Museum, Sofia

The Greeks put such faces on their shields, but also on household vessels, like the bronze water-jars from which the two Gorgons on this page are taken. The horns on the Gorgon above may show that she is a river-goddess.

Another Gorgon-mermaid, from a water-jar made in Corinth about 550 B.C., Bulgarian National Museum, Sofia

46

From a bronze fragment, c. 500 B.C. Museum of Fine Arts, Boston

From a sardonyx cameo, 3rd-4th century B.C. National Museum, Naples

This Gorgon's face, molded in clay and then baked hard, once decorated a temple in the Greek city of Gela in the south of Sicily. There were rows of faces like this one along the sides of the temple, hiding the ends of the roof-tiles above the gutter. Like the big Gorgon from Corfu, these faces were not just ornaments; in fact, you may think them very ugly. Their ugliness was meant to frighten away bad luck of all kinds.

From a terracotta roof decoration from Gela, 6th century B.C. Syracuse, National Archaeological Museum